# Butterflies

**WORKBOOK**

T0349870

HEINLE
CENGAGE Learning™

Y|S|G
A YBM COMPANY

Young & Son
Global, Inc.

# Building Background

● **Read and match.**

## How do these animals grow?

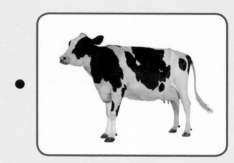

# Vocabulary Preview

● **Follow the lines. Trace and read.**

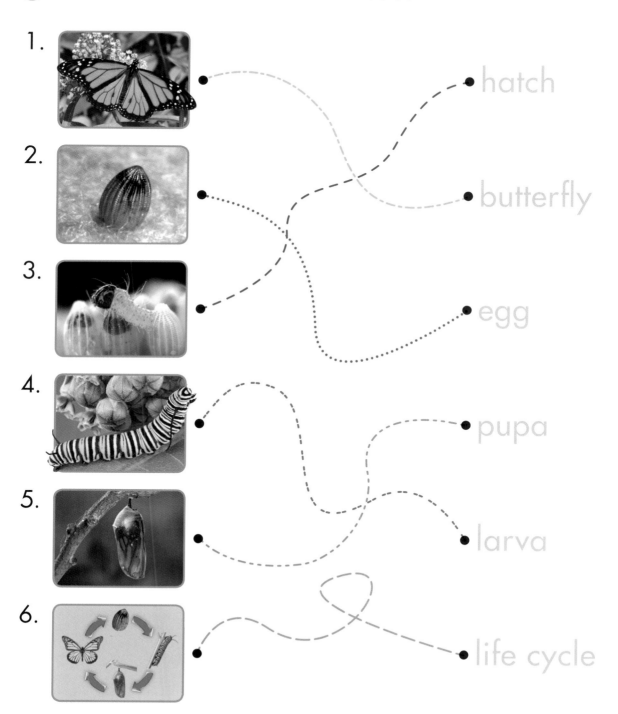

1. hatch

2. butterfly

3. egg

4. pupa

5. larva

6. life cycle

Look, read, and write.

| | | |
|---|---|---|
| egg | pupa | butterfly |
| larva | hatch | |

1. _____

2. _____

3. _____

4. _____

5. _____

# Key Sentence 1

● **Read and circle.**

1. The larva eats plants and grows bigger.

a.

b.

2. From outside, the pupa looks very still.

a.

b.

3. The fourth stage of the life cycle is the adult stage.

a.

b.

# Key Sentence 2

⬤ **Read, write, and match.**

| from | covering | butterfly | egg |
|------|----------|-----------|-----|
| pupa | starts | flies | larva |

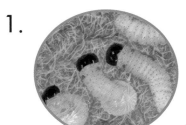

1. 

⬤      ⬤ A butterfly _____ its life as a(n) _____.

2. 

⬤      ⬤ A(n) _____ hatches _____ the egg.

3. 

⬤      ⬤ The larva makes a hard _____ and becomes a(n) _____.

4. 

⬤      ⬤ A(n) _____ breaks out of its covering and _____ into the sky.

# Reading Comprehension 1

**A** **Read and circle.**

1. This book is about _____.

   a. why butterflies fly
   b. how butterflies grow

2. The larva _____ until it is ready for the next stage.

   a. eats
   b. hatches

3. From outside, the _____ looks very still.

   a. pupa
   b. larva

**B** **Read and number the sentences from 1–4.**

How does a butterfly grow?

_____ From outside, it looks very still.
_____ It breaks out of its covering and flies into the sky.
_____ It starts its life as an egg.
_____ It eats plants and grows bigger.

● **Read and circle.**

1. The first stage of the life cycle is the egg stage.

True    False

2. The larva makes a hard covering.

True    False

3. The second stage of the life cycle is the pupa stage.

True    False

4. The larva eats plants and grows wings.

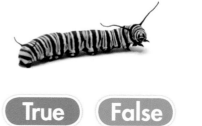

True    False

5. The butterfly can lay eggs and the life cycle starts all over again!

True    False

# Reading Comprehension 3

## A Read and circle.

1. What does a larva hatch from?
   a. An egg
   b. A pupa

2. Where does the larva attach itself before it becomes a pupa?
   a. To a flower
   b. To a leaf or a branch

3. Which of these can lay eggs?
   a. A larva
   b. A butterfly

## B Read and write.

What are the four stages of a butterfly's life cycle?

_____

_____

# Listening Comprehension

● **Look, listen, and circle.** 🎧 7

1.

    a.   b.

2.

    a.   b.

3.

    a.   b.

4.

    a.   b.

5.

    a.   b.

6.

    a.   b.

7.

    a.   b.

8.

    a.   b.

# Dictation

**Listen, read, and write.** (8)

1. A butterfly's _____ has four stages.

2. A butterfly larva can also be called a _____.

3. Then, the larva _____ itself to a leaf or a branch.

4. The third stage is the _____ stage.

5. Inside, the pupa slowly _____ into a butterfly.

6. The fourth stage is the _____.

7. Now, the butterfly can _____ and the life cycle starts all over again!

| | | |
|---|---|---|
| **life cycle** | **lay eggs** | **pupa** |
| **adult stage** | **changes** | |
| **caterpillar** | **attaches** | |

## Grammar

### ● Read, circle, and write.

1. A butterfly's life cycle _____ four stages.

   a. has                          b. have

2. How does a butterfly _____?

   a. grow                         b. grows

3. The larva makes a hard covering and _____ a pupa.

   a. become                       b. becomes

4. A butterfly breaks out of its covering and _____ into the sky.

   a. fly                          b. flies

5. Now, the butterfly can _____ eggs and the life cycle starts all over again!

   a. lay                          b. lays

# Sentence Practice

**Read and unscramble.**

1.

grows bigger    the larva

eats plants    and

_____

_____.

2.

the larva    attaches itself

then    to a leaf or a branch

_____

_____.

3.

a butterfly    the pupa

slowly changes into    inside

_____

_____.

# Graphic Organizer

⬤ **Reread "Butterflies" and write.**

**A Butterfly's Life Cycle**

A butterfly starts its life as a(n) _____.

A(n) _____ breaks out of its covering.

A(n) _____ hatches from the egg.

The larva makes a hard covering and becomes a(n) _____.

**pupa      egg      larva      butterfly**

| egg | butterfly |
|-----|-----------|
| larva | hatch |
| pupa | life cycle |